Blockchai Inte

How You Can Benefit from Blockchain Technology Beyond Bitcoin, Cryptocurrency, and Ethereum

Phillip Rawson

Table of Contents

Introduction 3

Chapter 1: What is the Blockchain? 5

Chapter 2: Brief History of Blockchain..................... 14

Chapter 3: Implements of Blockchain and Its Current Usage 18

Chapter 4: Advantages and Disadvantages/Dangers of Using Blockchain Technology.................................. 30

Chapter 5: Future Possibilities of Blockchain 36

Conclusion 43

Introduction

When the computer was first introduced to the world, it was difficult to imagine the heights that it would take us. The first of these devices to move us beyond the typewriter (which seems very antiquated in today's modern world) was a simple word processor that allowed us to type letters in a neat and compact fashion.

Fast forward to today. A world where information moves at the speed of light, people no longer have to leave their homes for shopping, to work, or even for entertainment. We are actually seeing the possibility that many common household conveniences we use now will one day be outdated, going the way of the typewriter, teletype, and the old-fashioned word processor.

It is hard to imagine a world where even these newfangled gadgets that we have come to rely on are also about to fade into the sunset. Enter Blockchain technology. It appears that once more, mankind is sitting on the edge of a revolution where our economy will have to go through another major transformation.

Here in this book, we're going to introduce you to some amazing facts about Blockchain. It does not matter if you have never heard of it and you will not need any special type of degree or education. The day is coming, and it is coming soon when everyone will have access to Blockchain and will be able to unleash the power that it holds within. Here we will answer questions like:

- What is Blockchain?
- How does the Blockchain work?
- How does the Blockchain use Bitcoin, Cryptocurrency, and other forms of digital currency?
- What is the future impact of the Blockchain on our daily lives?
- What are the advantages and disadvantages of the Blockchain?
- And what does the future hold for us?

If you have never heard about the Blockchain before, then this is a good place to start. A place where you can lay the foundation for your future and what you can expect in the days, months, and years ahead. So, let's get started.

Chapter 1: What is the Blockchain?

We live in fascinating times; technology runs through our veins just like the blood, we need to survive. In today's modern world, we can take advantage of incredible advancements that many of our grandparents could never even dream of. A time when with just a few keystrokes on your laptop, a few taps on your smartphone, or a few notes sent in an email can open untold doors. There is no question that with the invention of the Internet, life for humankind has taken a giant leap forward.

However, just like with everything in life, things are not always as good as they seem. While the Internet has provided us with a wealth of information and opened up a plethora of opportunities, these advancements did not come without their own drawbacks.

Now the Internet has reached the half-century mark, we have come to rely on it for nearly every aspect of our lives. Since its inception terms like the World-Wide-Web, social media, dot-coms, the cloud and such have become household words. Even if we do not have a computer in our home, there is a good chance that the Internet has managed a good portion of our lives. Medical facilities regulate our health, educational institutions use it to groom us for the future, and banks and financial institutions use it to keep track of our economy. In between all of that we use the Internet to communicate with friends and family, to be entertained, and to network with our businesses. Over the last fifty years, we have been a part of a major transformation where the Internet is the central figure.

So, many may wonder, 'what is the problem? If the Internet is all that, then why should we be looking for something better?' The answer is simple. It is not perfect. While a whole book can be dedicated to the flaws and weaknesses of the Internet, in this book we are only going to focus on one simple area. It impacts on the world's economy. It has been a miserable failure when it comes to protecting its users either financially or socially.

In the past, when you needed to communicate with someone else, you picked up the phone, dialed a number and spoke directly with that individual. Today, since most information and data is done online, there is limited direct interaction with live individuals. For the most part, we communicate almost entirely with machines. In the past, you walked into a bank and spoke to a teller who looked up your account information and gave you the money you needed. Today, you walk up to a machine, punch in a code, and a non-thinking machine dispenses cash to you.

In the past, we needed a middleman to verify whether or not we were whom we said we were. If you want to buy a house, a banker needs to verify your identity, credit history, and how much cash you have to invest. While the Internet has made that kind of data transfer much faster and easier, the world would literally come to a halt if the Internet ceased to function. The problem is this: We not only have had to develop a body of trust in the person we're doing business with but also in the middleman, leaving many of us more vulnerable than ever to an invasion of privacy, or open to one more person with their hand in our pockets. Why do we need to know that these third party individuals are trustworthy? Think about some of these facts:

1. Phishing/Spoofing: Even if your third party does prove to be trustworthy, they are vulnerable too to having information stolen. Phishing is when an unauthorized party accesses a company's computer and sends out emails or falsifies information to trick you into giving them your personal information they can then use to steal from you.

2. Blackmail/Extortion: This crime happens when someone threatens to use personal information in a way that could cause harm or damage to one's reputation.

3. Hacking: Intentionally gaining access to unauthorized information to use in many nefarious ways.

4. Identity Theft: In the past, for someone to steal your identity they needed to get some type of official document from you, painstakingly forge it, and then use it to their

advantage. However, now all they need to do is Google you, glean a few salient bits of information, use it to their advantage, and when they are finished, tear up the data they have collected and move on to the next victim.

The reality is simple: we have no idea whom we are dealing with when we interact on the Internet, and without the aid of that middleman, we are just hoping upon hope that the information we are trusting will end up in the hands of someone who cares to keep it to themselves. But the fact is that many of these people collect our personal information and without our permission sell it to the highest bidder opening the door for a host of new and more efficient cybercrimes perpetrated against us.

It has become increasingly apparent that a new system designed to protect the identities of those who use it and to cut out the middleman was needed. Over the last two decades, efforts have been made by many to take on this challenge, and those efforts produced positive results. These results became the platform for which the Blockchain was to be built on. Through this new technology, the average person can exchange currency for goods safely without the need of a third party.

The Blockchain is also a means of verifying information you may have collected through the Internet. It is an open source code, accessible to everyone at no cost. There's no question that the introduction of the

Blockchain can open up a world of new possibilities that can change the way many of us view the Internet, business, and the economy for years to come.

How Blockchain Works

One of the reasons why the Blockchain has become such a bright light on the horizon is because it allows users to exchange value without the need for a third party, reducing the risk of exposure to identity thieves, unwanted marketers, or any other people that would like to have access to your personal information. On the surface, it sounds pretty basic, but when you break it down into bite sized pieces, you can see how this can be very advantageous for all parties involved.

Probably the best way to explain it is with an example that all of us can appreciate. Let's suppose that you agree to have some work done on your bathroom with a local contractor. The amount of the transaction is very small, let's say it is less than $100.00. When it comes time to pay this transaction you as the payer have three options:

1. You say you are going to pay and the contractor has to trust that you will stick to your agreement. This system works if the two of you are both trustworthy. You trust that he will do a good job in your bathroom and he trusts that you have the money available to pay him when the work is done. However, with just an agreement, there is a

high risk that you could just not pay, and there is little the contractor could do about it.

2. You can enter into a contractual agreement, which is designed to protect both parties. With contracts, people are more inclined to pay for the services they have received because they do not want to end up in court. Still, for such a small amount, the cost of taking the matter to court may not even be worth the additional legal expenses they will incur.

3. Finally, you could bring in a third party to hold the money before the work is done. Once the work is completed to your satisfaction, the third party is notified, and they can issue the payment on your behalf. However, there is very little assurance that the third party will not take advantage of the knowledge they have gained about the agreement and use it to their own benefit.

As you can see, neither situation is an ideal solution for either party. In this day and age, it is difficult to know whom to trust. While you do have more security with a contract, there are still challenges with enforcing it.

The Blockchain provides a simple solution. By allowing you to input a few lines of code used by both parties you can transfer funds from one person to the other without the use of the third party. Each party can set up their own agreement, and once it is put in place, there is no changing it. The funds will be transferred to the other party once all parts of the agreement have been met.

While you may not have heard much about Blockchain, chances are you have heard about Bitcoin. This is a digital currency that allows people to exchange products and services. What many people do not realize is that Bitcoin is just one form of Blockchain technology. One Bitcoin (BTC) by itself has no particular value. However, its value is determined when we agree to use it in exchange for goods or services. As long as other people who use the Bitcoin agree on how much a BTC is worth, the value stays stable.

We keep track of how many Bitcoins a person may have by use of a digital file called a ledger. Unlike on the Internet, this ledger is not stored on a central server or data center. So, there is no single location where all this data is collected and maintained. Instead, it is distributed globally through a network of private computers responsible for storing data and making computations. Each of these private computer systems makes up a single "node" in the Blockchain and holds a copy of the ledger.

To pay your contractor for the work done in your bathroom, you send a message to this network telling them to reduce the number of BTC in your ledger by the amount you have agreed upon. At the same time, the amount of BTC in the contractor's ledger must go up by that same amount. Every node in the system will receive the message and make the necessary adjustments on the ledger they hold making sure that the account remains up to date.

To make these transactions, each user must have a "wallet," or a program set up to hold Bitcoins. The wallet is guarded with a cryptographic method unique to it, which uses a public and private key pair that is connected. Any message encrypted with a public key can only be decrypted by the owner of the private key in the pair associated with that particular wallet. So, to pay your contractor, you send out an encrypted message using the private key that you and only you can use to unlock the wallet and pay your contractor. Each time this passes through a node, it verifies that the transaction request is coming from you by checking against your key pair. Each time you make a transaction, you will use a different key pair so it can only be used one time, this way no one other than yourself can alter your transaction request or change the amount of Bitcoins being transferred.

A simpler way to think of it:

> To send money, you send your public key connected to your wallet. To prove that you are the true owner of the wallet, you need to use the private key to encrypt the transaction message.

It may seem just a little bit confusing. However, once you get the hang of it, you will find it much more secure and easier than regular bank transactions.

Chapter 2: Brief History of Blockchain

Like all other technologies, the Blockchain is quietly changing the way we do business and interact on the Internet. Considering all of its potentials, it may come as a surprise to know that the Blockchain as we know it is only a mere decade old. Let's consider a little about how this innovation has evolved over the years since its inception.

Bitcoin: While Bitcoin and Blockchain have often been used interchangeably, it is important to know that they are not exactly the same. Bitcoin was brought to life in 2008 when a published white-paper called Bitcoin: A Peer-to-Peer Electronic Cash System was published by an unidentified individual who used the pseudonym Satoshi Nakamoto.

In his paper, he claimed to have resolved the issue of double-spend by using a digital currency through a distributed database that utilized things like cryptography, game theory, and computer science. This allowed one individual or company to safely and confidently transfer value directly to another individual or company without the aid of a third party. In this sense, Bitcoin was the very first means of a digital medium that allowed a transfer of value from one person to another.

Up until 2010 the programmer who first introduced Bitcoin collaborated with some open-source developers on the Bitcoin program when there was a transfer of control to several prominent Bitcoin core developers. This transfer made it possible to eliminate the middleman in transferring funds by using the network itself as the intermediary. This system was used to verify transactions, and offer the assurance that no one could cheat the system by using the same Bitcoins twice.

The main purpose was to fill a void in the world of digital trust. Since money itself has no value unless both parties have agreed upon its worth the challenge was to determine how to build trust in the information one party gives to another about the worth of a product or service and what is considered to be an equivalent form of payment. Bitcoin has been able to do this by allowing users to operate entirely in a public forum by recording pertinent information in a public arena. This information cannot be removed making it that much harder to manipulate to one person's or group's advantage.

As the system continued to evolve, the Blockchain became more sophisticated by mixing some older technologies together. A good example of this is the use of cryptography and payment. We have learned through our history classes that cryptography has been around for thousands of years. It is the art of transferring information using a code. Payment, on the other hand, is the act of offering payment or value for goods or services received. When combined they fill an important role in the Blockchain called

Cryptocurrency, a completely whole new concept; the act of taking money and moving it via the Internet to exchange value.

Another feature introduced through the Blockchain is something called *hashing*. This is another twist on an old technology called Merkle Trees. These Merkle Trees take data of all sizes and transforms them into short, fixed-length values. They then take these short hashes and literally condense them down into one single hash, while at the same time preserving their ability to validate each piece of data that was originally hashed. In the end, each of these ancient technologies, when merged in the Blockchain creates a ledger that can be used to maintain an accurate record of finances.

At first, Bitcoin was developed as a means of transferring the Bitcoin cryptocurrency, but in a very short period, it was realized that it was just the beginning of something very big. It was then that they worked to expand the system to record and incorporate more data so that the system could transfer more value to other users. While Bitcoin is the first and also the largest Blockchain today, it consists of thousands of nodes that are actively safeguarding the network by mining for Bitcoin. Every day, new Bitcoins are collected for each transaction they process and record within the Blockchain. This is called "The Bitcoin Protocol."

Anyone can become a part of the Bitcoin Protocol and mine for these tokens because it is an open-source program that can adapt to the number of people using it. The more people use it, the stronger it becomes. The fact that these nodes are independent and distributed globally is the backbone that makes it a secure system and safer to use. Early on, all of this could be done on a home computer, but today it is necessary to use specialized equipment or to use a cloud service to mine for these Bitcoins.

To create a Blockchain message a user must transfer Bitcoin from one account to another. This message is openly broadcast throughout the entire network. Once the message is sent, it cannot be altered or changed in any way because it is now a part of the Blockchain. Therefore, it is imperative that creating your message is done carefully and that you take pains to avoid including any personal or sensitive data inside of it.

Once created, the message is forever part of the ledger and can never be removed. Still, it is a system that is constantly evolving, and we can expect more changes in the future. While anyone can become part of the Bitcoin Protocol simply by participating on the GitHub page (https://github.com/bitcoin) there is already a small community of core developers actively involved in spearheading the changes in the activity already done on the system.

Chapter 3: Implements of Blockchain and Its Current Usage

By now, we have already mastered the basics of the Blockchain, and we can easily see how Bitcoins have laid the groundwork for this new type of currency. However, as we stated before, while the two words are often used interchangeably, they are not the same. The Blockchain has a life that extends beyond the Bitcoin. In this chapter, we will look at several distinct implements of the Blockchain and how they work together to create the entire system.

On a very basic level, when we separate the Bitcoin from the Blockchain, what's left is the concept of a universal ledger that holds a running record of all transactions. So, at the heart of the Blockchain are various types of transactions and how they are recorded in these ledgers. How are they verified and applied to a wide range of situations? These are the basic functions of the various implements used in the Blockchain and understanding them can explain how they are used in all sorts of situations.

To understand this more fully, we need to look at each of these implements and see how they function as they preserve the quality of the data they send and receive, their level of accessibility, how they dispense and share the information, how it is encrypted, and they type of transactions they handle. As we go through the following pages, you will see how each of these implements address these and other issues a little differently.

Cryptocurrency

Just like in with any other currency, things are constantly changing. We have already learned that Bitcoin is a digital currency but it is not the only one, and while there are several types of this digital currency in use today, there are sure to be more created in the future to fill a particular need. As of the time of this writing, September 2017, the website https://coinmarketcap.com/all/views/all/ has listed more than 1100 different types of cryptocurrencies with Bitcoin being the first and the largest.

On the surface, it may seem a bit absurd to develop so many different types of currencies. Even the dental profession is in the process of launching its own form of currency called Dentacoin. While there are so many different digital currencies now used on the Blockchain, there are several that are key players in the system.

Type of Digital Currency	Market Cap
Bitcoin	$55 billion
Ethereum	$25 billion
Ripple	$6.8 billion
Bitcoin Cash	$5.1 billion
Litecoin	$2.3 billion
NEM	$2.3 billion
Dash	$1.4 billion
Ethereum Classic	$1.4 billion
IOTA	$1.3 billion

As you can see, cryptocurrency has become an integral part of the Blockchain with Bitcoin leading the pack. Generally speaking, when most people think of the Blockchain their minds will inevitably drift to the Bitcoin in much the same way as someone might think of Xerox when he or she wants to copy something.

Smart Contracts

One of the most attractive features of the Blockchain is the fact that the information it holds is not held in a centralized location. Because the information is dispersed globally, it saves you from having to trust a third party in your transactions and allows you to avoid paying extra fees for their services. This can be great news for anyone who is trying to make a financial transaction online. However, developers realized that they could take this a step further by implementing Smart Contracts.

With smart contracts, more things can be traded that go beyond money. Users can now trade property, shares in their stocks, or anything else of value they may have in a conflict-free manner without the aid of a middleman.

In normal everyday situations when you wanted to make an exchange you would enlist the aid of a notary, a lawyer, or some other professional, pay them a fee and wait for them to prepare the documents needed to effect the transaction. With Smart contracts though, you simply transfer a bitcoin to the ledger along with your escrow, identification or whatever documents are necessary to make the trade and it can all be handled right on the Blockchain. These Smart Contracts lay out the rules and the penalties connected to any agreement just like any other contract does and automatically enforces the obligations attached to it.

The process is simple:

- The Smart Contract is written into the Blockchain as a code. The parties involved are anonymous in the public ledger, but the contact and the transaction are recorded.

- A triggering event like a strike price, a due date, or an expiration date is set and the contract automatically activated according to the terms written in the code.

- Since the information in the code is on the public ledger, regulators can monitor activity in the market while the individual parties involved can still have their privacy protected.

It is easy to see how Smart Contracts can afford each participant with autonomy, trust, support, security, speed, savings, and accuracy all in one.

Ethereum

Because the world of cryptocurrency is constantly evolving things can change quickly from one day to the next. However, some digital currencies have maintained a relative level of stability and has seen few changes over time. Most people recognize Bitcoin as one of those stable currencies, but Ethereum is probably a close second.

Unlike Bitcoin, Ethereum is a digital currency that can also be used in conjunction with a Smart Contract. While Bitcoin works as a cash system, Ethereum has more extensive applications. Anyone can create applications that can support all sorts of trade. It works very similarly to your mobile device. Consider using a Smart Phone or a Tablet. These devices alone mean very little to a consumer but when equipped with a particular application (App) they can do all sorts of things. Like purchasing an app for your tablet, you can obtain a decentralized app (dApp) for Ethereum to do whatever you need to do.

From its very beginning, Ethereum has worked on the fundamentals of a Proof-of-Work model similar to Bitcoin. But now, Ethereum has switched to a Proof-of-Stake model. In their previous Proof-of-Work model, Bitcoin miners were required to invest in special equipment to solve a particular block in the chain. However, the Proof-of-Stake model being implemented on Ethereum uses validators instead of miners. A validator is allowed to stake a certain amount of their own money to solve a block. The more money they invest, the higher their chances of successfully solving a particular block. In essence, the funds they "stake" is like placing a bet.

Of course, with any type of gambling, there is a pretty high risk of someone trying to beat the system, but the Ethereum already has protections in place. If the system catches anyone trying to do something that is not in line with the protocol, they money they have staked will simply disappear, and they will be erased out of the system.

Both systems have the same goals in mind: to validate blocks and add them to the Blockchain in such a manner as to broaden the scope of the entire network. Both can accomplish this using different protocols, but Ethereum's new approach opens up other ways in which these new technological systems can be used in the future.

While you may not be interested in developing an application for Ethereum or planning on investing in this new platform, it pays to have a basic understanding of what is involved. Let's take a look at a couple of the dApps used on Ethereum to get a better picture.

Golem

The concept behind Golem is pretty basic. While many people have computers in their homes or offices, they do not use them continuously. Even when they are in use, they rarely take advantage of all of their processing power. As a result, there are massive amounts of computing power that is not being used. With Golem, people can "rent out" their unused computer processing power to those who may need it. People across the globe can make small quantities of computing power available to a huge computation task without the aid of a centralized network.

The Golem program is designed to create a decentralized supercomputer that everyone could have access to. Since the entire history of any program on the Ethereum Blockchain is fully recorded, users can be sure that no one can obtain more power than he or she have paid for.

Golem has its own digital currency that users can trade or invest in regardless of whether they are involved in a particular project or not.

Ripple

Ripple is another dApp found on the Ethereum platform. It has two purposes, 1) as a cryptocurrency and 2) as a technology company. While most transactions performed on the Blockchain are peer-to-peer trades with a concentration in the financial industry, Ripple is a bit more controversial. When using Ripple, it can eliminate the waiting period most people experience when verifying certain data. This way, transactions happen almost instantly.

The controversy lies in its use of a centralized network of servers. So, for the most part, the Blockchain's focus has been on decentralizing information, but with Ripple, the use of a centralized group of servers seems to defy logic. It ignores the overall concept of a distributed ledger, but for many investors, it is the key that can unlock the potential of the Blockchain.

FinTech

The term FinTech is derived from the combination of two words, financial + technology and applies to any type of innovation that manages how people transact business. Whether it is from the creation of a new type of currency or a prevention of catching double-entry bookkeeping. However, FinTech has grown over the years from these basic functions to include a wide number of technological programs that can be used both in personal and commercial finance.

In the past, people and organizations used the tools of the financial market to analyze and make decisions. However, now with FinTech much of the guesswork has been removed from such inadequate data pools. With new "learning apps" available through FinTech, they can not only learn the fundamentals that control and move the market, but they also have access to the behaviors of other users. They can learn about buyer's unconscious spending habits, get improved data analytics and more to help them to make better investment decisions.

In essence, FinTech is a means of facilitating daily financial decisions through disrupting everyday technology. It can be used with foreign exchange, online credit, and many other platforms to provide or obtain products or services that use both money and technology.

Companies that use FinTech take the place of the middleman on the world financial stage in a number of ways. They may transfer money, provide loans, or facilitate the purchase or the sale of securities. One common source of FinTech dApp is crowdlending companies, which bring together the small investor with small applicants in search of funding for their projects.

FinTech also facilitates money transfers across the globe, a service that previously could only be handled by large banking corporations.

FinTech objectives are simple:

1. To provide new financial services and the technical support needed to go with it.
2. To personalize and add value to the financial services already in use today.
3. To bring the world of financial trade completely online.
4. To lower today's expensive service fees.
5. To make financial services more accessible to more people with greater transparency.
6. To utilize more technology in solving problems related to financial services.

You will find that you are probably already using FinTech in your daily financial affairs. This type of dApp is most often found when you are using:

- Mobile Banking
- Crowdfunding
- Foreign Exchange
- Risk Management
- Making online payments and transfers
- P2P Loans
- Trading goods
- Insurance
- And much more.

As you watch the financial industry change, you will soon be able to recognize how portions of the Blockchain have already become a huge part of your life. It is only a matter of time before we will be witness to the rapid expansion of this new way of managing the world and everything in it.

Impact of Blockchain on Our Daily Lives and the World Economy

With every passing year, the world dips deeper and deeper into the digital age. Many of the practices that we used before the birth of the Internet have long outlived their purpose. Now, these will have to be incorporated into a new digital framework or fade away with the passage of time. We see much of that in other areas of our lives. Rather than sending postcards and writing letters, today we send emails and post pictures on social media, in essence reaching a host of people in a matter of seconds.

The Blockchain has the power to make that sort of change in our daily lives. There is no denying that the Blockchain will have a major impact on our future. Since nearly every aspect of our lives is already wired into the Internet (we already use GPS data to find our way, communicate through social media, interact with our financial institution, and buy and sell daily) we are already wired into the Internet on so many unconscious levels.

Chapter 4: Advantages and Disadvantages/Dangers of Using Blockchain Technology

There is no question that Blockchain technology is one of the most exciting innovations of this generation. The potential is high for turning the entire online world on its head. Whether you are an entrepreneur, a mom and pop shop, an investor, a worldwide corporation or a government official it is just a matter of time before you will be fully involved in this new technology.

We must keep in mind that this technology is still very new and as with all new things they come with a host of advantages and disadvantages that need to be considered. So, let's talk about some of these issues now.

Advantages

As you have already read, the advantages of the Blockchain are many:

- Transactions are simplified because now two parties can enter into an agreement, set the parameters for exchange without the use of the middleman. This will save loads of time and money in fees to third party institutions and reduce the risk of one party bailing on the agreement.

- Users can now be in control of all their information and transactions.

- The data collected through the Blockchain is more reliable and easy to obtain.

- Because the networks are not centralized, the Blockchain cannot fail at one single point. It has a much stronger defense from malicious attacks from nefarious people outside of the chain.

- It instills trust in the users as all transactions will be automatically executed according to the commands set down in the protocol.

- All additions to the public Blockchain are open to the public. Once in their system, they cannot be changed or deleted. They become a permanent part of the chain.

- Transactions can be made much faster as they have no days off. Transactions made on the Blockchain are done 24/7.

- Without the need of a third party, users save the cost of fees associated with value exchange.

Disadvantages

One of the major disadvantages of the Blockchain is the massive amount of data accumulated about each and every one of us that is floating around on the public platform. You might think that the Fitbit you use to monitor your daily workout, your social media pages, and your smart phones are all separate things but they all have a lot in common. They are all accumulating data about you, your personal life, your likes, and dislikes, etc.

If this information is not maintained in a centralized pool where does that data go and who technically owns it? Today, because the data is contained in a centralized location, companies can purchase your personal information and sell it to other companies for a price. Aside from learning how to target ads that appeal to you what other things might they want to do with you?

Let's look a potential example. Assume that today you go to the doctor and he uncovers a lump in your lung one day. He tells you not to worry too much about it, but when you leave, you turned on your search engine and spent several hours perusing different websites to find out what could possibly be the cause. Unbeknown to you, an online company has just gained access to your online search, and they notice that you also searched for a specialist in cancer screenings. You also did some research on updating your life health and life insurance (just in case). With all this information, what could they do with it? What are the implications for you?

This is supposed to be a private matter between you and your doctor, but professionals may use that information against you. For example, your insurance provider may use the information to raise your health insurance rates or your bank could infer things that could affect whether or not you get your homeowner's loan. These are, of course, extreme examples of what could happen when all things are transparent and open for every eye to see.

The more integrated our lives become when we use this modern technology, the more ethical and legal questions will have to be answered. Once data is collected who owns that data and under what conditions should it be released and to whom? People want to know all sorts of things about us; the music we listen to, the movies we watch, our shopping habits, our political affiliations, and even our sexual preferences will become a matter of public speculation if this type of streaming is not managed and regulated. So, the question that must be foremost in our minds is whether our private information is better off in the hands of a centralized system or spread across the globe in small bits and pieces.

Another possible disadvantage of the Blockchain is that with the absence of the middleman in executing transactions, could open the door to higher criminal activity. As we become more deeply entangled on the Internet, more and more people will be seeking to find ways to control the environment and act in ways that will implicate them criminally. This is directly connected to each individual's rights to privacy, their personal welfare and their every day lives. As the Blockchain permeates into our personal lives beyond financial matters, it is beginning to attract a lot of attention and inevitably will invite a whole new type of criminal activity that we may not be prepared for.

Those are the two most obvious drawbacks to the Blockchain, but there are others:

- While transactions can be done quickly, the amount of time needed to verify the situation can slow the process down considerably. Many websites also have data limits, which could limit the amount of time it takes to complete a transaction.

- While much of the Blockchain has yet to be regulated, you can bet that like all other currencies, governments and financial institutions will be seeking ways to manage and regulate or even tax the transactions that are conducted through this new system.

- Statistics show that the Bitcoin Blockchain miners are working on an average of 450 thousand trillion solutions every second. This uses untold amounts of computer power. Probably one of the largest consumptions of energy in the world.

- Finally, for the Blockchain to take hold, it will require the entire globe to rethink how transactions are done. Regardless of culture, background, economic position, or hierarchy, everyone will have to view transactions in a completely different way making for a huge learning curve that will need to be overcome.

Let's face it. The new Blockchain technology is quite exciting but at this stage is without regulation and guidelines. It is like the Wild-Wild-West out there. It is a time to explore the new frontiers ahead of them. There's no telling how far this will go in the future.

Chapter 5: Future Possibilities of Blockchain

As we enter into this unexplored territory, we will find a lot of potential for the future. Some of it we have already considered, and others have yet to be uncovered. Keep in mind that wherever there is room for growth, there is also a high risk for those who dare to step out into the unknown. Already we see large technology companies like Samsung, IBM, and Uber already getting into the mix. Below is a list of a few things that we could realistically expect to see in the very near future.

- As more financial institutions adopt the Blockchain and incorporate it into their businesses, more cryptocurrencies will be traded globally.
- Nasdaq will soon launch a digital technology that can be used to enhance the Nasdaq Private Market.
- Using the Blockchain ledger to authenticate identities will require more technology to lower the risk of cybercrime.
- Smart Contracts will be used by car rental agencies to verify insurance and the availability of payment.
- Small businesses could incorporate the Blockchain to build trading platforms with other peer businesses.
- There will be more transparency when conducting business.

- With the right dApp, government agencies could use the Blockchain to track down criminals faster than ever before.
- Even governments and NGOs could use the Blockchain to distribute needed food and materials to less developed countries or to disaster areas more quickly.

Not only do we have access to one of the most innovative ways to manage currency the world has ever seen, but there are also endless possibilities that have yet to be thought of. The Blockchain is on the precipice of a new tomorrow, and at some point, we will all play a part. There is a lot of room to grow, and the full potential for this new program has yet to be seen.

What Blockchain Can do for You

While there is a big, beautiful, and wonderful future waiting ahead for the Blockchain, you do not have to wait until then to reap its benefits. There are things that you can do, right now, today, on the Blockchain. Some of them you probably already know about and others you may be surprised to learn. Below is a list of things you can start doing today on the Blockchain.

1. Transfer money. Right now you can bypass the third party banks and their fees by transferring digital money through the Blockchain.

2. Micropayments: You can now transfer small amounts of money to any place in the world. In fact, some dApps allow you to transfer amounts as small as a fraction of a cent to another user. All of these without incurring large bank fees for the privilege.

3. Lend money: With peer-to-peer lending now possible, users can make an even larger return on their savings by offering low-interest loans to other users with the use of Bitcoins or another form of cryptocurrency.

4. Pay fines: Some cities now allow car owners to pay their fines via Bitcoin.

5. Share utilities with your neighbors: Some streets in a neighborhood may get more sun than other streets. Those with solar-powered homes can transfer their excess power to those who may need it. Rather than selling your power back to the utility company, you can now transfer that excess power directly to your neighbor saving him money and making a tidy little profit for you.

6. Verify your identity: You can now dispense with the government paperwork to prove who you are. Now you can manage your own credit history and prove your identity to

employers, banks, or any other agency you may be dealing with.

7. Prove you are the owner of an asset: With vehicles, the government maintains a list of license plates or VINs you can use to verify that you are the true owner of an asset. However, other assets cannot be regulated so easily. Portable assets like jet skis, bicycles, or even your Gucci handbag can be quickly moved from one area to the next with no way to really trace them. The dApp, Mamoru, is designed to provide a global record of proof of ownership.

8. Make an equity trade: With a Smart Contract, you can use the Blockchain to make a peer-to-peer trade of equal value goods.

9. Register a copyright: Artists can now use the Blockchain to register their own copyright for their work.

10. Cast your vote: Because of Blockchain's transparency, there is now an adaptation for casting your ballot in the next public election. Countries like Estonia are now allowing shareholders to vote on changes in their corporation and are in the process of developing e-voting machines for both state

and national elections that can work on the same principle.

This list can go on to include many more things you can do with the Blockchain. Whether you want to register your land rights, establish a legal contract, or manage your healthcare, the Blockchain probably has a dApp designed to meet your own unique needs.

How You Can Profit from Blockchain

There are several ways you can make a profit from using Bitcoin technology. All of them are simple and easy to do once you learn the ropes. However, several factors need to be considered before making the switch from traditional investments. Your choice of investment will depend largely on your personal circumstances, the level of risk you want to undertake, and the type of return you want to earn. Here are just a few suggestions:

1. Stockpiling Bitcoin: Bitcoin can be accumulated and stockpiled in much the same way as one would stockpile gold. As the value of the Bitcoin continues to rise the profit potential will also increase. Since there is a ceiling limit of a total of 21 million Bitcoins, the amount of profit to be had can only increase with the demand.

2. Penny Stocks: There are also penny stocks available as an alternative form of cryptocurrency. Many have been specifically designed to fill voids in the digital world that the Bitcoin left behind. There are many opportunities for investing in Blockchain penny stocks.

3. Crowdfunding: A very popular means of raising capital for a variety of investments, crowdfunding is now a mainstream strategy to generate funds for all sorts of opportunities.

4. Angel Funding/Startup Ventures: You can now invest in a new startup company built entirely with Blockchain technology. By providing the startup funding, you can become a principal figure in groundbreaking new ventures. Who knows? You might become a part of the next Apple or Microsoft.

5. Blockchain Technology Play: Many companies are becoming major players on the Blockchain scene. Many strategically place themselves as part of the Blockchain infrastructure offering verification services or other technology that is needed to keep the chain flowing smoothly. Investing in these companies can make you an integral part of the whole system yielding all sorts of profits.

These are just a few examples of how you can earn a profit from the Blockchain. There are many more opportunities out there to choose from. Your choice will depend on your appetite for profit, how much risk you are willing to take and the time line you have available. The good news is that there are many ways you can earn a pretty good profit from the Blockchain if you do your homework.

Conclusion

Whether you want to use the Blockchain as an investment tool or you are more interested in its convenience, one thing is for sure, The Blockchain is here to stay, and it promises to be a very important part of our future economic system. Still, there is a lot more to learn about the Blockchain than what is written in these pages. As a final note, here are just a few simple tips to smooth your way until you can get a good grasp on Blockchain Technology.

1. **Privacy:** People trade billions of dollars every day on the Blockchain without your knowledge. On the surface, you know that your financial dealings should only involve those you are transacting business with. However, the digital ledger is highly transparent, so all transactions are a matter of public knowledge. This can leave you susceptible to some nefarious characters who may not have the best of intentions. You need to set up a system to distinguish between honest business affiliates and hackers. Here are three things you need to do when interacting on the Blockchain.

    A. Use a proxy
    B. Browse
    C. Use a VPN (Virtual Privacy Network)

Proxy Security: We have been using proxies for a long time. It is simply a method of setting up a location where users can send a connection through so that the end user cannot distinguish your exact location.

Virtual Private Network: Using the VPN is a perfect way to preserve your privacy. Because VPNs are encrypted when you use them your online activity is also encrypted. Your whole system will be hidden, so you never have to worry about keeping the activities you engage in private.

2. **Learn as Much as You Can:** Get as many resources as you can find to learn all you can about the Blockchain. There are now schools that give you hands on training and teach you all the ins and outs of the Blockchain. Take nothing for granted; the more you learn, the easier it will be to grasp, and the more profitable your transactions can be.

3. **Keep Good Records:** At the very least, you want to record what you need to recover your wallet in case something happens. You need to know your wallet ID and the password. Keep this information stored in a place where you can get it if you need it. Back up your wallet whenever possible and make sure that you have a record of your public and your private key in a separate location.

4. **Have More Than One Wallet:** You can have as many wallets are you want. Never put all your eggs in one basket, have a different wallet for every type of transaction to ensure that you are not putting all your assets at risk.

5. **Use Malware or Virus Protection:** Just because your computer is housing all of your information and it is not kept on the World-Wide-Web does not mean that you are entirely secure. For protection, nothing beats a good antivirus program. Always store your back up information in an offline platform. You can still encrypt it with a private key that will require decrypting just in case it falls into the wrong hands.

In these short pages, we have discussed many things. Getting a good understanding of the Blockchain can be a challenging task. It requires that we think about how we acquire goods, use currency, and make trades in a totally new and innovative way. But hopefully, through these pages, we have sparked your interest enough to delve a little deeper into this whole new world of digital currency. If we have, then the next step is obvious. It is time to get busy and find your place in this new platform called Blockchain technology.

Milton Keynes UK
Ingram Content Group UK Ltd.
UKHW050809240724
445899UK00013B/467